POWER BASICS OF
BASEBALL

POWER BASICS OF
BASEBALL

Bill Polick
Ed Lupton

Prentice-Hall, Inc.
Englewood Cliffs, New Jersey

Prentice-Hall International, Inc., *London*
Prentice-Hall of Australia, Pty. Ltd., *Sydney*
Prentice-Hall Canada Inc., *Toronto*
Prentice-Hall of India Private Ltd., *New Delhi*
Prentice-Hall of Japan, Inc., *Tokyo*
Prentice-Hall of Southeast Asia Pte. Ltd., *Singapore*
Whitehall Books, Ltd., *Wellington, New Zealand*
Editora Prentice-Hall do Brasil, Ltda., *Rio de Janeiro*
Prentice-Hall Hispanoamericana, S. A., *Mexico*

© 1985 by
Bill Polick
Ed Lupton

Library of Congress Cataloging in Publication Data

Polick, Bill
   Power Basics of Baseball.

   Summary: Top athletes and coaches teach
the fundamentals of baseball.
      1. Baseball—Juvenile literature.   [1. Baseball]
I. Lupton, Ed   II. Title.
GV867.5.P65   796.357'2   84-18331

ISBN 0-13-688292-7

Printed in the United States of America

The Early Beginnings

Sunday in New York in the early 1840s usually found a group of young men getting together to play a game they called "town ball." The game was so called because it was played on town meeting day. In some places it was called "round ball," aptly named after the British game of rounders. You might also hear the name "sting ball" or "burn ball" used to distinguish the game simply because the players threw at the runner before he reached the safety of a post or a base.

If hitting a player with a ball wasn't bad enough, just imagine running into one of the posts while trying to dodge the ball.

In those early days, the rules (which barely existed) changed from town to town, and variations of the game prevented any real team play unless it was right in a player's block.

Then, about 1843, on a Sunday, a tall, broad-shouldered young man approached some friends who were about to start their game of town ball. Gathering them around him, he began to show them his design for a new game, a game he would later call "baseball."

Alexander Cartwright had not only conceived a strategy for his new game but had also prepared a set of rules to guide the players.

Four bags (or bases) were used instead of posts. The four bases were marked off on a field and were forty-two paces apart. Instead of hitting the runner with the ball, a runner was put out by letting the ball arrive at the base before him or simply by being tagged by the ball. Other changes included allowing only three outs and having competing sides try to score twenty-one aces, or runs, which would win the game. Each team had equal times at bat (innings) to try to score.

Cartwright's design did much to speed up the play and also made the game more fun to watch. Alexander Cartwright had set the beginnings for organized baseball.

There were many other changes made before the game was turned into what resembles present-day baseball. Calling strikes and balls, changing the game to nine innings and nine players on a side, pitching overhand from a greater distance, and deadening the ball were some of these changes.

In 1849, Alexander Cartwright heard about the gold strike in California and decided to head west. As the wagon train moved along, Cartwright taught the settlers and Indians the fundamentals of his game of baseball. When he reached California, he was dissatisfied with life in that area, and after a short time he sailed to the Hawaiian Islands. There, with his guidance, the passion for baseball grew faster than it had on the mainland.

By the 1860s, baseball had grown enough in popularity to be considered a national pastime. Different businesses in each city would put together teams, with some towns having over fifty clubs. The Steam Fitters Union, the cotton mill employees, the local department store workers—everyone seemed to be playing baseball.

Then in the late 1860s, the Cincinnati Red Stockings became the first professional team, and many others soon followed. By the mid-1870s, baseball was being played in Japan. In the late 1800s, a U.S. touring team played in Italy, England, France, Ireland, and even Egypt.

Just as there were changes in the rules of the game, the equipment was also modified with these changing rules. In the early days, ball players had to buy their own uniforms. The heavy flannel material used in these uniforms became even heavier and more unbearable because it absorbed the players' perspiration on hot days. When the material was washed, it also shrank. Thus players would begin their season in over-sized baggy uniforms in order to compensate for the shrinking. A lighter-weight flannel shirt was later used, and the addition of rayon made the uniforms less heavy and cooler.

Straw hats, used in early days were replaced by flat-topped caps similar to those now worn by the major league Pittsburgh Pirates. These caps and shirts were made up in colors to identify a particular position. By 1883 color was limited to the players' stockings, with the rest of the uniform being in the team color, or simply in white. Numbers appeared on the backs of shirts in 1916, and by 1930 all professional teams were using them.

Baseball shoes were originally made of canvas and later made of leather, with toe and heel plates attached for protection. Not too much has changed with spikes, other than some of the modern-day spikes are made from a synthetic material. In the 1890s the manager of the Cleveland Spiders had his players file their spikes in order to inflict injury on their opponents. There are now rules that protect players from such tactics, and safety for the player is of great importance.

Originally, the catcher would allow the ball to bounce before catching it. By 1901 however, the catcher moved to a position right behind the batter. Knee pads and scrap pieces of cloth stuffed into stockings did little to protect the catcher from foul tips and from the spiking by a runner trying to score. By 1907 shin guards similar to those used in cricket were introduced. Because of the lack of face protection, it was very common for a catcher to have no teeth. A mouth protector was later used, followed by a fencing mask. The most recent modification has been a flap connected to the lower part of the mask (under the chin) to protect the neck.

Baseball originally was played bare-handed. The first glove was nothing more than a piece of leather covering the hand, leaving bruised and broken fingers exposed. The glove was turned into a padded mitt as more padding was stuffed into the palm of the glove. The mitt was first used only by the catcher and the first baseman. In 1892 a catcher who was switched to third base decided to keep using his glove. This caused great controversy at the time; apparently it was believed that the game would be spoiled if all the fielders used them. In the end the padded glove prevailed and has been on the road of modification ever since.

Bats and baseballs have also seen some dramatic

changes. Ash is a common wood for making bats, but hickory was also used in early games. Bats are cut into forty-inch lengths and are allowed to dry naturally for up to two years. After a bat is removed from the lathe that cuts it, it is flame-treated. This hardens the surface. Professional players sometimes treat their own bats as well. Pine tar can be wiped on the bat with rags to create a sticky grip. In early games the players were more concerned about the length of a bat than its weight, but now weight is measured to the ounce, and dimensions are very specific; even the grain of the wood is important to the hitter.

The many modifications of the ball have created continual controversy. In early years, teams with little power used large, soft balls, and the powerful teams would use just the opposite, depending on who was on the hometeam. The balls were limited to two per game, and a new ball could only be used in the beginning of each inning. If both balls were lost in the course of one game, the game had to be forfeited. In more recent times, the complaint has been that the ball is livelier, making home runs easier and earned run averages higher.

In spite of all the changes that have taken place over the last one hundred plus years, what has made baseball the great game it is now has been the hundreds of players and personalities who played the game with excellence. Today we have Pete Rose almost ready to break Ty Cobb's major league record of 4,191 hits. The epic home runs by Babe Ruth, Hank Aaron, Mickey Mantle, and Roger Maris will never be forgotten. Players with names that sounded like jingles, such as "Three Fingers" Brown and "Wee Willie" Keeler, were stars in their time.

There are also unbelievable feats of achievement, such as the day Joe Oeschger and Leon Cadore each pitched twenty-six innings before they settled on a 1–1 tie. Tom Cheney struck out twenty-one batters in a sixteen-inning game. There are inspirational records, such as Lou Gehrig's playing 2,130 consecutive games or Ted Williams' lifetime batting average of .344 or the year Walter Johnson had a 36–7 win-loss record as a pitcher for the Senators.

The baseball greats are too many to list. Their achievements could fill several books. What can be said is that they lived and loved the game of baseball to its fullest.

In the chapters that follow, we will give you a solid foundation for becoming a truly excellent baseball player. For whatever the future may hold, be it as a sports superstar or a superfan, we feel the *Power Basics of Sports* (Baseball) book will give you a greater understanding of the game and make it more enjoyable.

The Cast

Dick Williams

Jerry Reuss

Terry Kennedy

Garry Templeton

Kurt Bevacqua

DICK WILLIAMS

Dick Williams is recognized as one of baseball's top managers, with over 1,200 victories in his sixteen years as a major league manager. His reputation for turning players into winners is backed by his two World Championships with the Oakland A's, and by his American League Championship with the Boston Red Sox. He has been chosen Major League Manager of the Year in both leagues. He made the Montreal Expos pennant contenders, and he is now doing the same with the San Diego Padres. With over thirty years of professional baseball experience, his winning philosophy makes players believe in themselves.

JERRY REUSS

Jerry Reuss has been the top Dodger pitcher for several seasons. His pitching consistency has put him among league leaders in several categories. To date he has one no-hitter and two one-hitters to his credit. In 1980 he was runner-up for the Cy Young Award in the National League and was also selected to the National League All-Star team that same year. Jerry was the winning pitcher in game five of the 1981 World Series against the New York Yankees. He is a student of the game and a master in the art of pitching.

TERRY KENNEDY

Terry Kennedy is the catcher for the San Diego Padres, and is also a two-time National League All-Star. In 1983 he was the best hitting catcher in the National League. His .285 National League career batting average ranks him as one of the best hitting catchers playing the game today. Terry began his career in the St. Louis Cardinal organization. Since becoming a San Diego Padre, his batting average has been around .300, and he also has the reputation for being an excellent defensive catcher.

GARRY TEMPLETON

Garry Templeton makes playing shortstop look easy because of his grace of movement. He combines his outstanding defensive ability with equally impressive offensive skills.Garry has led the National League shortstops in runs, RBIs, game-winning RBIs, and has tied for second in stolen bases and in triples. He is the first switch-hitter in major league history to collect one hundred or more hits both right- and left-handed in one season. He has played on two National League All-Star teams, and is now the starting shortstop for the San Diego Padres.

KURT BEVACQUA

Kurt Bevacqua finished the 1983 season as one of baseball's top pitch-hitters, with a .412 batting average. He is a pressure ballplayer who has the ability to get hits with runners on base. Not only can Kurt drive in runs, but he can also help the team by playing several positions. The versatility of Kurt Bevacqua is a positive asset for any championship team. He is now in his thirteenth season and is playing for the San Diego Padres.

Contents

POWER BASICS OF
BASEBALL

1

Pitching

Jerry Reuss

Pitching is broken down into three very important elements. The first element is location. You have to put the ball exactly where you want it. The second element is movement on the ball. That's what confuses hitters and makes them unsure of where the ball will cross the plate. The third element is velocity of the ball. Varying speeds on your pitches also keeps the hitter guessing.

If you think of these three things while you're on the mound, if you've prepared yourself properly with long hours of practice, you stand a good chance of success.

chapter 1

Windup and Delivery

Dick Williams
Being a pitcher means being the most active player on the team during a game. You are involved in every play, and because of that you have to be in good physical condition and be able to control your emotions.

THE MOTION

Jerry Reuss

Because pitchers are so active during a game, it is important that they be comfortable on the mound. When you look at the catcher for the sign, relax and concentrate. In Picture 1 you see that I am standing on the rubber with my arms semirelaxed and that I am concentrating. In a typical game, I will throw over one hundred pitches, so it is important to remain relaxed whenever I can.

Once you get the sign from the catcher and know whether you are going to throw a fastball, a breaking pitch, or a change-up, you are ready to begin your windup. The first step is always backward, as in Picture 2. Remember to keep one foot on the rubber, and as you step back, you are building momentum, which will help you develop your drive to the plate.

Be sure to keep your hands high enough so that you still have a full view of the target. In Picture 3 you can see that as I kick my leg, I have my eyes riveted on the target, and I know exactly where the ball has to go. My foot is still in contact with the rubber, but I have rotated my foot from the top of the rubber to the side so that my cleats do not catch during the delivery. My hips have rotated slightly, and I am using a high kick of the leg to continue the momentum.

Picture 1

Picture 2

Picture 3

Even though some pitchers in professional baseball deliver the ball without maintaining eye contact with the target all the time, it is a habit they learned a long time ago and have learned to deal with. It is not a recommended skill, and that is why so few pitchers do it.

THE FOLLOW-THROUGH

Jerry Reuss

Once you have made the pitch, you become a fielder, so it is important to follow through properly.

As you release the ball, you have to end up in a position where you are ready to catch a ball, cover first base, or back up a play. To do that, come down with your eyes on the ball and watch the hitter. Keep your weight as balanced as possible so that you will be ready to move in whichever direction the play dictates. Since you are the closest fielder to the ball, you have to be ready to react quickly once the ball is hit.

In Picture 4 you see me just after I have delivered the ball and am getting into position to field the play, if necessary.

Picture 4

As a pitcher you should make sure your body works as a single unit. Your arms, legs, head, shoulders, and hips should all contribute to the delivery.

HITTING THE SPOT

Jerry Reuss

One of the reasons you should keep your eye on the target is so that you can hit it with more accuracy. The catcher will almost always give you a low target, and that is for a reason. Very few hitters can drive a low pitch very far; the one that is down in the strike zone keeps a hit low and is more likely to become an out or a single. High pitches end up as doubles or home runs.

chapter 2

Hiding the Ball

Dick Williams
One of the things you are trying to do as a pitcher is to deceive the hitter, to not let him know what you are going to throw or where you are going to throw.

KEEP THEM GUESSING

Jerry Reuss

As a pitcher you have to develop a rhythm and at the same time find a way to upset the hitter's rhythm. All the batter is trying to do is hit what he sees. But you can fool the batter.

There are several ways to do that. You can throw different pitches by varying speeds or by throwing breaking balls. You can also come from different directions by coming overhand one time, three-quarters the next, and you can also add an occasional sidearm toss now and then.

An effective way of keeping the batter guessing is to not let him see the ball before you release it. Hide the ball in your glove and behind your body. Hitters are smart. If you hold the ball where they can see it, they can see what grip you have on the ball and will be able to tell what kind of pitch you are going to throw. If a batter knows you are going to throw a certain kind of pitch, he can wait for it, and you lose the element of surprise. If he doesn't know what is coming, the chances of his making contact are less.

How do you hide it? Simple. Keep your glove or body between the ball and the batter. In Pictures 5 and 6, you will see how I am doing it. Notice in these shots that I am gripping the ball in the mitt and that there is no way for a hitter to see it. If I were to bring the ball too far behind my head, it would be

Picture 5

Picture 6

exposed so that the hitter could see it. The back of the glove should face the batter.

At some point in your delivery, the ball will have to come out of the glove, and then it is time to keep your body between it and the hitter. In Picture 7 you can see that a student has the ball effectively hidden, even though it is out of the mitt.

Picture 7

If you are having difficulty hiding the ball when you bring it behind your head in the windup, try stopping at the top of your motion; don't go so far back. Once you are comfortable with that, try going back more and more until you find a good position.

chapter 3

The Grip

Dick Williams
How you hold the ball determines what kind of pitch you will
throw. There are three basic pitches: the fastball, the curve
ball, and the change-up, and each has a different grip and
release. Although there are different pitches, it is important
to find the grip for each pitch that is most comfortable for you.

THE FASTBALL

Jerry Reuss

I like to throw two different kinds of fastballs, one that moves toward a hitter and one that moves away from a hitter. These are not curves, they simply tend to tail away from the batter while they retain their speed.

The grips of my fastballs vary. The first one uses four seams of the ball rotating; the more seams rotate, the more movement there is on the ball. In Picture 8 you can see that my first and second fingers are together *across* the seams, and my thumb is on the opposite side of the ball. The pitch is released with no twist of the wrist so that when my fingers let go of the ball, it rotates with four seams.

The second type of fastball I throw uses two seams rotating. In Picture 9 you will notice that my first two fingers are still together, and my thumb is still on the opposite side of the ball for support, but my fingers run *with* the seams this time. I release it the same way as the other fastball, but since there are only two seams rotating, the motion is different; in fact, it actually tails off in the opposite direction.

Picture 8   **Picture 9**

THE CURVE BALL

Jerry Reuss

The curve ball is a very effective pitch because it makes the hitter wonder if the ball is really going to be where he thinks it will be.

Curve balls are also four-seam rotation pitches, but the grip and release are different from the fastball. Look at Picture 10. Notice that I am holding the ball on one seam as I do for the second fastball, but my fingers are horizontal instead of vertical. When I release the pitch, the middle finger pulls the ball through, the index finger guides the ball against the inside part of my hand, and when I release the ball, it rolls off my fingers. This gives the four-seam rotation. the better the spin, the more rotation on the ball.

Picture 10

THE CHANGE-UP

Jerry Reuss

Pitchers over the years have developed several change-ups including the palm ball, the knuckleball, and the fork ball. The idea is to make the hitter think the ball is coming in at one speed when it is actually coming in slower.

The secret of a good change-up is to make the hitter think that the pitch is a fastball by using the same motion. By holding the ball differently, your arm and body work the same, but the pitch comes in slowly. My change-up uses the four-seam rotation. I hold the ball against the palm of my hand, grip it with three fingers instead of two, and hold the fingers across the seams, as in Picture 11.

There is no way that I can throw a ball held like this as fast

Picture 11

as a fastball, but the hitter doesn't know that.

Remember, the key to a successful change-up is deception; make it look like what it is not.

chapter 4

The Pickoff

Dick Williams
The pick-off is a valuable defensive tool. It takes away a
potential run, it takes pressure off the players in the field, and
it leaves an impact on your opponents.

GETTING THE OUT

Jerry Reuss

At some point in a baseball game, you will probably
have a runner on first base, and you will have to decide
whether you are going to hold him on or try to pick him off.

In this situation you will use the stretch position instead of
a full windup. Put your foot next to, but touching, the rubber.
Get the sign from the catcher; then start your windup. You will
hesitate when the ball gets to your waist. At that point you will
look at the runner.

If you decide to throw the ball to the first baseman, you
must step toward the base and throw, as in Picture 12. If you
step toward first and throw home, or if you step toward home
and throw to first, you will be charged with a balk, and the
runner will be allowed to go to second base. Remember to both
step and throw either to home or first base.

After a while the runner will be able to figure out your
timing and know whether you are going to pitch or throw to
first. Therefore, it is important to develop variety in your timing
to keep the runner guessing. To do this, you can look back and
forth between first and home several times, or you can step off
the rubber and throw to first base, as in Picture 13. If you take
your foot off the rubber, you can throw to the base without
stepping toward it.

Picture 12   **Picture 13**

When you have developed your move so that the runner cannot figure out where you are going to throw the ball, you will have a better chance of throwing him out.

KEEP THEM CLOSE

Jerry Reuss

If you are just trying to keep a runner close and are not afraid he will steal, you should also vary your pattern to the plate. For example, you might use a high leg kick on one play, as in Picture 14, and a lower kick on the next pitch, as in Picture 15.

Picture 14

Picture 15

Right-handed pitchers have one advantage that we left-handers don't have. The runner cannot see your hands, so he has something else to think about and cannot tell exactly what youare going to do.

If you are right-handed, you will have to look over your left shoulder to see first base, as in Picture 16. If you don't see the runner out of the corner of your eye, he probably has too big a lead, so you should throw over to first.

Picture 16

Remember that most bases are stolen off the pitcher, so it is important to vary your delivery and throw over to first as often as necessary to keep the runner close.

chapter 5

Covering the Position

Dick Williams
*Pitching is not just throwing the ball; it is defense as well. To
be a good pitcher, you have to be able to do more than just
throw the ball accurately.*

COVERING FIRST

Jerry Reuss

One of the most common mistakes young pitchers make is
on defense. When the ball is hit toward the first baseman, they
break immediately toward the bag. This, of course, puts them
on a collision course with the runner and can lead to a serious
injury if the players collide at the base.

When you must cover the base, the first thing you should
do is break for the baseline then run toward the base, as in
Picture 17.

Picture 17

Picture 18

Picture 19

By the time you reach the bag, you should have the ball and then should tag the inside corner of the base, as in Picture 18. If you tag the bag in the middle or on the outside, you stand a chance of having your foot stepped on by the runner, so touch the inside of the bag and then remove your foot quickly.

If, for some reason, the first baseman bobbles the ball, then you have to play as if *you* are the first baseman. Run to the bag in the normal manner, plant your feet, stretch, and take the throw, as in Picture 19.

FIELDING THE BALL

Jerry Reuss

When the ball is hit so that you can make the play, you have to know how to get the runner out.

The first thing to do is get over to the ball, as in Picture 20. Once you have the ball under control, plant your feet and turn, as in Picture 21. Then throw the ball to the first baseman, as in Picture 22.

Remember that when you are making the defensive play, you have to come quickly off the mound and control the ball.

Picture 20

Picture 21

Picture 22

chapter 6

A Special Power Basic

Dick Williams

Baseball is a game you can play almost anywhere, from the beach or sandlot to modern stadiums in major cities. But whether it's two boys playing catch or eighteen professionals battling for the World Series Championship, it's still a game of fundamentals.

You have to practice long and hard to do anything well, and baseball is a perfect way to master skills that will help set examples for many years of your life.

chapter 7

A Power Basics Checklist

Windup and delivery

Be comfortable on the mound.
First step is backward.
Keep one foot on the rubber.
Keep your eye on the target.
Follow through so that you can field the ball, if necessary.
Keep the pitch low.

Hiding the ball

Vary your delivery to keep the hitter guessing.
Hide the ball so that the batter cannot see it.
Keep the glove or your body between the ball and hitter.

The grip

The more seams that rotate, the more motion on the ball.
Fastballs are thrown straight overhand with either two- or four-seam rotation.
Curve balls are four-seam rotation, with the middle finger pulling the ball.
Change-ups are held with three fingers, with the ball against the palm.

The pickoff

Vary your move.
Vary your rhythm.
Right-handers should see runner out of corner of eye.

Covering the position

Run to the line, then to the first base to cover.

If the first baseman bobbles the ball, plant foot, stretch, catch ball.

If you are fielding, control ball, plant feet, turn, throw.

2

Batting

Terry Kennedy

I think when you're hitting, the most important thing is to get as many good swings as possible. Your goal is to hit the ball hard somewhere so that you can get on base or drive in runs, depending on your position in the lineup.

I don't always try to hit home runs, but if the game requires it, I'll go for the fence.

chapter 8

The Stance

Dick Williams
Being a successful hitter means being comfortable at the plate and executing the fundamentals. Making contact with the ball comes only after mastering the basics, and they begin with the stance.

GETTING COMFORTABLE

Terry Kennedy

The first step to getting comfortable at the plate is to find a bat that suits you. You don't want one that is too heavy or too light (Picture 23). If a bat is too heavy, you will not be able to get it around quickly enough on a fastball; if it is too light, it may throw off your timing.

Once you find the right bat, step into the batter's box and find a comfortable position in relation to the plate. You don't want to be too far away so that you cannot reach the outside of the plate, and you don't want to be too close so that the pitcher can jam you on the inside corner. The best way to measure the distance is to stand in the box, hold the bat straight out, then lower it to the plate. If the bat touches the outside of the plate, as in Picture 24, then you are in good position, and you can reach the outside of the strike zone. If the bat touches any other part of the plate, adjust your position.

Picture 23

Picture 24

FEET AND LEGS

Terry Kennedy

When you step in the box, spread your feet to a comfortable position, not too close together or too far apart. In Picture 25 you see the position that is most comfortable for me; my feet are a little wider than my shoulders. If your feet are too close together, you have to stride too far to hit the ball, and if they are too far apart, you cannot get enough of a stride to put power into your swing.

Picture 25

HAND POSITION

Terry Kennedy

It is important that your hands be in a comfortable position. This is a matter of personal choice. For some players the best spot is with the bat straight up, for others it is with the bat over the shoulder at an angle of as much as ninety degrees.

Be sure not to put your hands too far behind your body, as in Picture 26, because it takes too much time to swing through the ball. If your hands are too far in front of your body, as in Picture 27, you will not have enough stroke and will not be able to put much power into the ball.

Picture 26

Picture 27

THE STRIDE

Terry Kennedy

Striding is simply taking a step toward the ball, but its timing is very important. As the ball is coming toward the plate, you stride and just after your foot hits the ground, your hands should come through the strike zone. You have to practice to get the timing and coordination down pat, but once you do, you will find that it becomes second nature.

chapter 9

The Pivot

Dick Williams
Hitting requires more than just swinging your arms and hands. It is a skill that uses the whole body working together. Your hips, legs, and feet must work in coordination with your upper body for the maximum power in your stroke.

DRIVING

Terry Kennedy

When you are hitting, it is important to use your lower body properly. As you begin your swing, you should drive with the back leg and keep your weight on the inside of your feet, as in Picture 28. It is almost as if you are standing knock-kneed.

Picture 28

This allows you to drive with your back leg and stop your stride with your front foot.

When you stride and swing, don't bend your front knee; start with your body squared to the pitcher, as in Picture 29. You should also make contact with the ball while your hands are still behind your front foot. Stay squared until you see the pitch, then commit yourself and swing.

Picture 29

SPIN ON THE TOE

Terry Kennedy

Just striding as you are swinging is not enough. Be sure to spin on the toe of your back foot, as in Picture 30. This will rotate your hips for better extension, and the hips will throw your hands naturally toward the ball, as in Picture 31.

Once you have made contact with the ball, follow through smoothly, as in Picture 32.

Using this system, you will not have to worry about your hips; they will automatically follow the rest of the movement of your body.

Picture 30

Picture 31

Picture 32

chapter 10

Eye on the Ball

Dick Williams
How many times have you heard a coach yell to the players to keep their eyes on the ball? Obviously you cannot hit what you do not see, so you must watch the ball if you want to hit it.

WATCHING THE BALL

Terry Kennedy

Even in the major leagues, the most important fundamental of hitting is looking at the ball. Since the pitcher will do everything possible to fool you, it is important to study him and know his motion (Picture 33).

Picture 33

The first thing you should do is determine the pitcher's release point, the spot at which he lets the ball go. This will enable you to pick up the ball as soon as possible. To learn the release point, watch the pitcher warming up or throwing to other hitters.

After you learn the release point, you should see the ball quickly and follow it all the way to the point of contact with the bat, as in Picture 34. Never take your eye off the ball before you hit it. Pitches are coming at you very fast, and looking away for even a split second can mean the difference between a hit and a strike.

Picture 34

LOOKING AT THE POINT OF CONTACT

Terry Kennedy

Once you hit the ball, don't follow it with your head; keep looking at the point of contact, as in Picture 35. If you try to follow the ball off the bat, chances are that you will look away too soon. It is also important to keep your head still. Don't bob around.

I know it sounds impossible, but try to see the ball hit the bat. If you do that, you have a better chance of keeping your head down and keeping your eye on the point of contact.

Practice hitting as often as you can because the more skill you develop, the more you will be able to hit.

Picture 35

chapter 11

The Swing

Dick Williams
Swinging a bat through the strike zone means a lot more than just moving a bat toward a ball. There are certain fundamentals in the swing that must be mastered before you can be as effective as possible.

A BAT IN THE HAND

Terry Kennedy

Breaking your swing down into the basic elements will help you understand what you are doing and will improve your motion.

The first thing to learn is that the knob end of the bat should lead your hands. You can see what I mean by looking at Picture 36. The knob should point toward the pitcher as your

Picture 36

arms move forward and then move toward you as you make contact with the ball.

The head, or thick part, of the bat should always remain even with or above your hands. Look at Picture 37 to see what I mean. If the head drops below your hands, as in Picture 38, you are more likely to hit pop-ups.

Picture 37

Picture 38

COMING THROUGH

Terry Kennedy

Hitting the ball is a lot like chopping down a tree with an axe. You use the same action. When you actually hit the ball, the hands should be square with the line of the ball, as in Picture 39. As you make contact with the ball, rotate your hands.

Picture 39

THE FOLLOW-THROUGH

Terry Kennedy

The finish of the swing, the follow-through, is really not that important, but you should not make any radical moves. It should merely be the continuation and end of the swing. Once you have made contact with the ball in the hitting zone, the hands turn over, and the bat continues through its natural arc, as in Picture 40.

Picture 40

chapter 12

The Bunt

Dick Williams
One of the most potent offensive weapons a team can have is a good bunter. A well-placed bunt in the right situation can win games, advance runners, and keep the defense wondering.

THE SACRIFICE BUNT

Kurt Bevacqua

There are two types of bunts in the game of baseball, and each is used for a specific purpose. There is the bunt for a base hit and the sacrifice bunt. The names accurately reflect the goal of each: The bunt for a base hit is as good a strategy as a grounder up the middle, and the sacrifice bunt means that you sacrifice yourself in order to advance a runner to the next base.

You can make a sacrifice bunt good by placing the ball almost anywhere between the foul lines except right at the pitcher. To start, stand in the batter's box until the pitcher is in his windup and then square around to face him. At the same time, slip your top hand toward the label of the bat, as in Picture 41. This will give you the control you need to drop the ball on the ground. Try to get the ball to hit toward the end of the bat because that is the area that will make the ball die. If you hit it too hard, it will roll quickly to a fielder, and the sacrifice will not work.

Picture 41

The high pitch is the toughest to bunt because the ball has a tendency to hit the top of the bat and pop up into the air.

Be sure to get your eye down near bat level and watch the ball into the bat and hit the ball down. Aim the ball down the baseline, if possible, as in Picture 42. If you hit the ball too hard, or hit it toward the pitcher, the defenders will have a better chance of throwing out the runner you are trying to advance. In Diagram 1 you see the ideal locations for the sacrifice bunt. Remember that the defense will probably be expecting a sacrifice bunt, so it is important to aim the ball carefully so that the fielder will have to throw to first to get you out and not be able to throw out the lead runner.

Picture 42

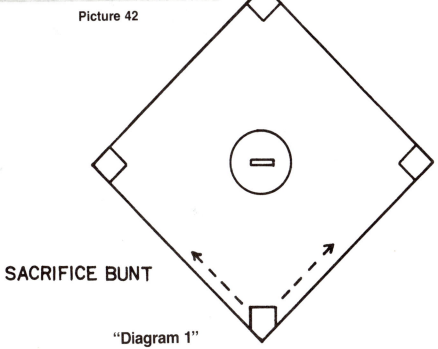

SACRIFICE BUNT

"Diagram 1"

BUNTING FOR A HIT

Kurt Bevacqua

Bunting for a base hit is a little different from a sacrifice bunt. If you look at Diagram 2, you will see the positions to bunt for a hit. You can still aim the ball down the third base line, but instead of aiming down the first base line, you should aim the ball more toward the second baseman.

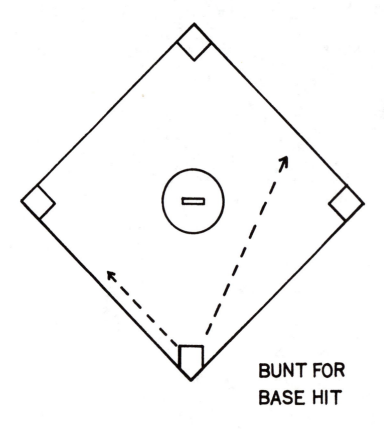

**BUNT FOR
BASE HIT**

"Diagram 2"

The bunt down the third base line should be within three or four feet of the line so that neither the pitcher nor the third baseman can get to the ball quickly. This is an effective area if the defense is playing deep and not expecting the bunt. If you aim on the other side of the infield, try to get the ball between the first and second baseman and aim for the edge of the infield grass.

When you bunt, make sure you aim your bat carefully and make contact with the ball in front of the plate.

Bunting is an important skill, and you should practice it as much as possible.

chapter 13

A Special Power Basic

Kurt Bevacqua

I don't look at pinch-hitting as only one chance to hit. I get myself ready while I'm still on the bench so that when the manager calls on me, I know what the game situation is. I know what the pitcher's throwing because I've been watching.

When you're pinch-hitting, you have to be ready mentally as well as physically and have a lot of self-confidence. You have to think you're the best player in this position and not look at how hard it's going to be to get a hit, but rather how hard it's going to be for the pitcher to get you out.

You have to maintain a positive attitude if you are going to succeed as a pinch hitter.

chapter 14

A Power Basics Checklist

The stance

Get a comfortable bat.

Find a spot where your bat tip will touch the outside of the plate.

Feet should be a comfortable distance apart.

Step toward the pitcher when you swing.

Hands should be comfortable.

The pivot

Drive with your back leg.

Put weight on inside of feet.

Spin on the back toe.

Eye on the ball

Determine pitcher's release point.

Follow ball to point of contact.

Keep looking at point of contact after you hit the ball.

The swing

Knob of bat leads hands.

Bat head should remain even with or above hands.

Rotate hands only after contact.

The bunt

Sacrifice bunt advances runners.

Bunt ball anywhere between foul lines but not at the pitcher.

Move upper hand toward bat label.

Square toward the pitcher.

Bunt for base hit should go toward second baseman or
third base line.

3

Field Action

Garry Templeton

You don't have to be fast to be a good base runner; you just have to be smart. I've seen guys who couldn't run a lick, and they were the best base runners because they always knew how the pitcher worked and where the defenders were playing. They knew how fast they were, and they also knew how well each player on the opposing team could throw the ball.

chapter 15

Baserunning

Dick Williams
Baserunning is just as important as any other skill in the game of baseball. It is a "head's-up" part of the game, which requires concentration as well as good reactions.

GETTING READY

Garry Templeton

Once you reach a base, it is time to pay attention to what you will do next. The first thing you have to do is watch your coach for the sign, as in Picture 43. It is very important to know what the coach is telling the hitter to do so that you can be ready. The coach may want to play hit-and-run, or want you to

Picture 43

try to steal the next base, so you must pay attention to what the coach signals.

Once you know what play is on, you should look at the defensive players to see where they are positioned, as in Picture 44. You should already know basically what each of the players on the other team can do, and once you see where they are, you will know how to advance if the ball is hit.For example, if you are on first base and the ball is hit on the ground to the right fielder, you should know if he has a strong enough arm to throw you out if you try to get to third base.

Picture 44

THE LEAD

Garry Templeton

The lead you take is a matter of individual choice. You should get as far off the base as possible, but keep in mind that the pitcher may try a pickoff play, so you have to be able to get back quickly (Picture 45). In the following section I will explain in more detail how far off base you should be.

Picture 45

GETTING TO THE NEXT BASE

Garry Templeton

After you get your lead, keep your eye on the batter and watch what is going on. The instant the ball is hit, you should take off for the next base, but if the ball is hit in the air, you should stop about halfway to the bag and watch to see if the ball is caught. If it is, you must turn around and get back to your base quickly.

The first step you take when the ball is hit is what we call a crossover step. Pivot on your right toe and step across your body with your left foot. Never shuffle. Make a deliberate move.

When the ball is hit, run to the next base; don't go straight at the base. As you get about halfway, veer out slightly. Go out just enough so that you can round the base with a good turn and determine whether you can advance farther. For a good example, look at Picture 46.

Picture 46

Always look at the coach when your are running the bases. He is there to watch the ball for you and to judge whether you can make it farther or not. Since he is facing the ball, he knows where it is, where the defensive players are, and can signal you.

chapter 16

Stealing

Dick Williams
Base stealing has become a real art in the last few years.
Major leaguers such as Maury Wills, Lou Brock, and Ricky
Henderson have stolen more than one hundred bases in a
single season and have added a great offensive weapon to
their teams.

THE LEAD

Garry Templeton

Stealing a base is very important. If you can get to second or third base without the benefit of a hit, you are in a much better position to score once the ball is hit. If you steal second, you can probably score on a hit to the outfield; if you make it to third,. you can score on a sacrifice fly. In fact, if you are on third with less than two outs, you can score seven different ways that you could not from another base: a walk, passed ball, wild pitch, sacrifice fly, squeeze play, error, stolen base! The first thing you need to be a good base stealer is a good lead, one that puts you as close to the next base as possible, but one that will allow you to get back to your bag if the pitcher throws the ball in a pickoff attempt. In Picture 47 you can see the lead I like to take.

Most successful base stealers take a three-step lead. Stand on the base and take three steps toward the next base. This allows you to step back toward the bag in one step and touch it with the next, as in Picture 48. If the play is really tight, you can also dive back to the base easily.

Once you have your lead, get your body in a comfortable position. Put your feet about shoulder-width apart with your weight balanced.

Picture 47

Picture 48

KNOWING WHEN TO GO

Garry Templeton

Before you can steal a base, you have to "know" the pitcher, you have to recognize when he is going to throw to the plate or when he is going to try a pickoff. Watch the pitcher, and as soon as he makes a move to home, take off. Drive your left arm across your body, as in Picture 49. This helps keep your body low. You don't want to stand up too soon; in fact, you should stay low until you are about halfway to the next base, as in Picture 50.

Pump your arms and start with choppy steps, as in Picture 51. You should start just as a sprinter does leaving the blocks. You, of course, will make your first step a crossover.

When you are trying to steal a base, don't veer out as you would on a hit, run straight to the base, as in Picture 52.

Picture 49

Picture 50

Picture 51

Picture 52

HINTS ON PITCHER-WATCHING

Garry Templeton

You might think it is easier to steal off a right-handed pitcher than a lefty, but it is actually just the opposite. Because a left-hander is facing you, he can see you better, but you can also see him better and know what he is going to do. Since the right-hander has his back to you, it is more difficult to know where he is going with the ball.

Picture 53

Picture 54

With a right-handed pitcher on the mound, watch his front leg. In order for him to go to the plate, he has to move his left knee, what we call "break," as in Picture 53. Once you see the break, it is time to take off.

Left-handers face you, and you can see their hands, legs, eyes, and motion better (Picture 54). As soon as you see a pitcher going to the plate, take off.

chapter 17

Catching

Dick Williams
Catching may be the most physically demanding position on a baseball team. Squatting behind the plate for nine innings is uncomfortable at best and dangerous at worst. Catchers are involved in almost every play; they are nicked by foul balls, and they have to wear awkward equipment to protect themselves. And yet there are very few catchers who don't like what they do.

THE STANCE

Terry Kennedy

As a catcher you must find a stance that both is comfortable and allows you to move around. Not every pitch will be directly into your glove, so you have to be able to get to the ball.

To get into the proper stance, stand behind the plate with your feet a little wider apart than your shoulders; then crouch, as in Picture 55. From this position you can go to the right or left or block balls in front of you. Keep your rear end up a little; if it is too low, as in Picture 56, you cannot move as well. Put your weight on your toes and keep your elbows out a little.

THE SIGN

Terry Kennedy

Part of your job as a catcher is to tell the pitcher what he should throw by giving him a sign with your fingers. To do this

Picture 55

Picture 56

Picture 57

properly, you should put your glove hand on your knee, as in Picture 57. This helps block the sign from the view of the third base coach. Give the sign high up between your legs so that your right leg blocks the view of the first base coach.

CATCHING THE BALL

Terry Kennedy

Once you have passed the sign to the pitcher, your next job is to give him a target. Keep your glove low, as in Picture 58. Remember what Jerry Reuss said in Chapter 1: "Very few hitters can drive a low pitch very far; the one that is down in the strike zone keeps a hit low and is more likely to become an out or a single. High pitches end up as doubles or home runs."

As the ball comes to the plate, rotate your glove slightly. This will relax your arm and let it move quickly.

Picture 58

THROWING OUT THE RUNNER

Terry Kennedy

One of your assignments as a catcher is to try to throw out runners who are trying to steal a base. You have a good view of the runner no matter what base he is on, and you will see him break toward the next base as the ball is coming to the plate. As soon as you see him take off, step forward with your right leg, as in Picture 59.

Catch the ball with two hands and take the hands, glove, and ball across your letters to the throwing area, as in Picture 60. Stand up and stride with your left foot, and keep your eyes on the base, as in Picture 61. Throw the ball through the bag and aim it at the chest of the player who is covering.

Picture 59

Picture 60

Picture 61

chapter 18

Ground Balls

Dick Williams
Playing defense, and playing it well, in the game of baseball requires a thorough knowledge of fundamentals. Fielding ground balls may seem a simple task: Watch the ball, bend over and pick it up, throw. But it is a lot more; it is a skill that requires techniques learned through practice.

PLAYING THE INFIELD

Garry Templeton

When you are playing the infield, you must always be alert. You have to know where the ball might go, and if it comes to you, you have to know where you will throw it.

Watch the batter, know what the play should be before you get the ball, know where runners are, how many outs there are, and where your teammates are playing.

Infielders have to be comfortable in their positions. Start with your feet shoulder-width apart, weight balanced, knees slightly bent, glove down so that if the ball is hit hard, the glove is already in position, and your head up so you can see the play and look the ball into the glove. Look at Picture 62 for an example of the correct position.

When the ball is hit in your direction, move in front of it, and as it appproaches, make sure your bare hand is over the ball. If you are in the correct position, you can get the ball with ease. If the ball should take a bad hop as it nears you, you can block it with your bare hand or with your body.

Be sure to stay low; if you have to come up, as in Picture 63, you can. It is much harder to lean over for a ball than it is to stand up to get it.

Picture 62

Picture 63

If the ball is hit softly, move quickly toward it. Don't hang back and wait for it to come to you. Once you have it, know where to throw the ball and throw it quickly and accurately.

PLAYING THE OUTFIELD

Kurt Bevacqua

The most common play for an outfielder to make is picking up a ball hit through the infield. Your job is to get the ball and throw it to the cutoff man.

Once the ball gets through the infield, the second baseman or shortstop will come out toward the ball in a position to cut off the throw. Once you throw it to him, he will relay it to another player.

Just as Garry said about the infield, the outfielder has to get in front of the ball, as in Picture 64. Stay relaxed; if you tense up on a play, you stand a greater chance of misplaying the ball.

Picture 64

You have to block the ball with your body. Balls on the outfield grass can take bad hops, so you need to be ready for them. The basic position is the same as the outfield, but don't be afraid to drop to one knee to block the ball (Picture 65). It is better to be cautious than to make a mistake.

Picture 65

chapter 19

Fly Balls

Dick Williams
Catching fly balls sounds easy enough: The ball goes up, it comes down, you catch it, you throw it. But knowing how to get to the ball, knowing how to catch it, and knowing where to throw it are important skills you must learn.

INFIELD POP-UPS

Garry Templeton

As an infielder you already know that you watch the batter on each pitch. When the ball is popped up into the infield, you have to keep an eye on it. If it comes in your direction, watch it, as in Picture 66. If you are wearing sunglasses, flip them down to help you see the ball better.

Picture 66

If you are going to catch the ball, your first step should be backward. I know that may sound strange, but you step back to help align yourself with the ball. Once you are in position, move up to the ball for the catch.

It is a good idea to catch the ball on the side of your body, as in Picture 67. This allows you to see the ball all the way into your glove. If you hold the glove in front of your face, you will not be able to see it. If your glove is over your head, you will not see it either, and it is difficult to catch what you cannot see.

Picture 67

OUTFIELD FLIES

Kurt Bevacqua

Catching flies in the outfield is only slightly different from in the infield. You have to learn how to judge where a ball is coming down (Picture 68).

You must also know what the ball will do after it is hit. As an example, you are playing left field, and there is a right-

Picture 68

handed hitter at the plate. He hits a fly ball in your direction. Chances are the ball will come straight in the direction you are playing. BUT if the hitter is left-handed and he hits the ball to left field, there is probably going to be spin on the ball because he did not hit the ball at the right point. The ball will probably tail off toward the left foul line. If you are playing right field, the same thing holds true in the opposite direction; that is, right-handers' flies will tail off to the right foul line.

It is important for you to know these facts so that you can move in the proper direction to catch the ball.

I recommend catching the ball on the throwing side of your body, as in Picture 69. When you catch this way, the ball is already in position to begin the throw. If you catch it on the other side, you have to bring the ball all the way across your body before you can throw.

Once you catch the ball, throw it to your cutoff man (Picture 70). In the game of baseball, a split second can mean the difference between having an opponent out or in a scoring position.

Picture 69

Picture 70

chapter 20

A Special Power Basic

Garry Templeton

One of the problems you have to face as an infielder is that not all balls that are hit in your direction are right at you. You have to move to one side or to the other to get them.

The technique I use to get these balls is to start just as if I am stealing a base. I throw my arm across my body as I break to the ball, and it has really given me much better range.

Kurt Bevacqua

When you are playing in the outfield, you have to know everything you are going to do ahead of time. Know what you are going to do if the guy hits a double, a single; know where you will throw the ball. The most important thing to do is hit the cutoff man.

chapter 21

A Power Basics Checklist

Baserunning

Watch your coach for the sign.

Look at defense positioning.

Take a comfortable lead.

Stop halfway if the ball is hit in the air and watch what happens.

Use a crossover step.

Veer out slightly as you approach the base so that you can round it.

Stealing

Use a three-step lead.

Feet should be shoulder-width apart.

Watch the pitcher.

Drive your arm across your body, stay low.

Pump your arms, take choppy steps.

Go right to the base.

Catching

Get into a comfortable stance.

Keep rear end up.

Block the view of the signs, give them high between legs.

Keep the target low.

Rotate your glove slightly as ball approaches.

Step forward when runner leaves, to prevent stolen bases.

Catch ball with two hands and bring them across letters.

Stride and keep eyes on base while aiming at baseman's chest.

Ground balls

Watch the batter.

Feet shoulder-width apart.

Glove down.

Look ball into glove.

Bare hand over ball.

Block ball with body.

Go down on one knee, if necessary.

Fly balls

First step is back.

Move to ball.

Catch ball on throwing side of body.

Know where the ball will go; will it tail away?

Throw to the cutoff man.

Epilogue

Baseball has been and will remain a sport that is watched and played by millions of people in the United States and millions of people outside the United States.

Girls are now playing as actively as boys in school or for recreation. The high caliber of play in the colleges is equivalent to playing in the minor leagues. Players who don't go on to play at professional levels will most likely become the avid fans of the game. Some play the game for many years as amateurs.

Dick Williams, manager of the San Diego Padres, has made champions of players and has managed teams to division titles and to World Series Championships. He is a man known for his knowledge of every aspect of the game.

As Dick Williams says:

Baseball is a game of confrontation, a constant battle between the pitcher and the batter. In my thirty-seven years of baseball, I've learned that it's the player who best executes the fundamentals that wins the game. If you love the game as much as I do, you want to know as much about the basics of playing the game as possible. Whether it's two boys playing catch or eighteen men battling in the World Series, it is still a game of fundamentals. Now is the time to start learning and practicing your hitting, your pitching, you baserunning, and your fielding.
